TABLE OF CONTENTS

1. **BAKED CHICKEN WITH GRAVY**
2. **FRIED CHICKEN**
3. **SALMON CROQUETTES**
4. **CAJUN POTATOES W/SAUSAGE, PEPPERS, AND ONIONS**
5. **ONE PAN MACARONI AND CHEESE**
6. **PARMESAN CRUSTED COD FISH**
7. **LEMON PEPPER WINGS**
8. **BAKED CHICKEN THIGHS W/A LEMON DIJON SAUCE**
9. **HOMEMADE CHILI**
10. **BEEF AND MACARONI**

BAKED CHICKEN W/GRAVY

SERVINGS: 6   PREPPING TIME: 30 MIN   COOKING TIME: 70 MIN

INGREDIENTS

- 1 tbsp Chili Powder
- 1 tbsp Paprika
- 1 tbsp Black Pepper
- 1 tbsp of Salt
- 1 tbsp of Thyme
- 1 tbsp of Cayenne Pepper
- 1 tbsp of Garlic Powder
- 1 -10 oz can of Cream of mushroom soup
- 1 -10 oz can of Cream of Chicken soup
- 1 cup of Chicken Bone Broth
- 1 Red Pepper (cut Julienne style)
- 1 Yellow Pepper (cut Julienne style)
- 1 Onion (cut Julienne style)
- 2 lbs of Wingettes

DIRECTIONS

1. Season your chicken with the paprika, black pepper, salt, thyme, cayenne pepper, and garlic powder.
2. Pour the bone broth into your roasting pan.
3. Place the chicken into the roasting pan.
4. In a separate bowl mix the cream of chicken and cream of mushroom soup together.
5. Place that mixture on top of the chicken. Fill any gaps you see with the mixture.
6. Place your sliced onion, red pepper and yellow pepper on top of the chicken.
7. Cover with foil
8. Bake in the oven at 375 degrees for 45 minutes.
9. Remove from the oven and remove the foil.
10. Bring the chicken to the top with a fork. Placing the veggies underneath.
11. Season the chicken with chili powder.
12. Place back into the oven at 415 degrees for 25 minutes.
13. Remove and serve.

FRIED CHICKEN

SERVINGS: 6   PREPPING TIME: 20 MIN   COOKING TIME: 30 MIN

INGREDIENTS

4 cup of Flour

1 cup of Water

3 tbsp of Seasoning Salt

2 tbsp of Cayenne Pepper

3 tbsp of Garlic Powder

2 lbs of wingettes

Vegetable oil

DIRECTIONS

1. Mix 1 cup of flour with 1 cup of water into a large bowl.
2. Season that mixture with 1 tbsp of seasoning salt, 1 tbsp of cayenne pepper, and 1 tbsp of garlic powder.
3. Add your wingettes to the wet batter. Make sure to submerge the chicken so that they are coated in the mixture.
4. For the dry batter, in another large bowl mix 3 cups of flour with 2 tbsp of seasoning salt, 1 tbsp of cayenne pepper and 2 tbsp of garlic powder. Mix well.
5. One by one, roll each with from the wet batter into the dry batter and place onto a rack. Let the rest for 2 to 3 minutes.
6. Fry the wings at 350 degrees for 12 minutes and they are golden brown. Enjoy.

SALMON CROQUETTES

SERVINGS: 6 PREPPING TIME: 20 MIN COOKING TIME: 30 MIN

INGREDIENTS

1 Onion (diced)

1 Green Pepper (diced)

2 cans of Pink Salmon

1 egg

2 tbsp of Flour

1 tbsp of Yellow Cornmeal

1 tbsp of Seasoning Salt

1 tbsp of Black Pepper

1 tbsp of Garlic Powder

2 cups of Vegetable Oil

DIRECTIONS

1. Sauté the onion and green pepper and set that to the side.
2. Place the pink salmon into a bowl. (Optional - remove the bone)
3. Add the egg, flour, cornmeal, seasoning salt, black pepper, and garlic powder. Mix well.
4. Form the patties with your hands. Compress them so that they stay together. Form 12 patties from the mixture.
5. Pour your oil into a hot pan on medium heat.
6. Once your oil is at 350 degrees, brown the patties on each side for 3 to 5 minutes. Enjoy!

CAJUN POTATOES W/SASAUCE, PEPPERS, AND ONIONS

SERVINGS: 6   PREPPING TIME: 20 MIN   COOKING TIME: 45 MIN

INGREDIENTS

- 1 lb of Smoked Sausage
- 1 Onion (cut Julienne style)
- 1 Green Pepper (cut Julienne style)
- 1 Red Pepper (cut Julienne style)
- 1 cup of Olive Oil
- 2 tbsp of Cajun Seasoning
- 2 tbsp of thyme
- 2 tbsp of garlic powder

DIRECTIONS

1. Slice your sausage into bite size pieces.
2. Dice your potatoes into bite size pieces.
3. Season the potatoes with cajun seasoning, thyme and garlic powder.
4. Mix in 2 tbsp of olive oil and make sure the potatoes are evenly coated.
5. Pour olive into a hot pan and brown your sausage.
6. Remove your sausage.
7. Add your potatoes to the pan and saute for 3 to 5 minutes.
8. Add your veggies and saute for another 2 to 3 minutes.
9. Lower the heat, cover and let simmer for 30 minutes.
10. Add your sausage back to the pan. Mix in well. Enjoy.

ONE PAN MACARONI AND CHEESE

SERVINGS: 6　　PREPPING TIME: 5 MIN　　COOKING TIME: 20 MIN

INGREDIENTS

- 1 box of large macaroni noodles
- 2 tbsp of Chicken Broth
- 2 ounces of Velveeta Cheese
- 1/2 cup of Grated Parmesan Cheese
- 1/2 cup of Shredded Cheddar Cheese
- 2 tbsp of Sour Cream
- 1 tsp of Seasoning Salt
- 1 tsp of Paprika
- 2 tbsp of butter

DIRECTIONS

1. In a hot pot on medium heat, pour your noodles into the pan.
2. Pour enough water in the pan to just cover the noodles.
3. Stir for a few minutes.
4. Add the chicken broth and stir.
5. Once most of the water has evaporated add your Velveeta Cheese.
6. Stir until the cheese melts
7. Add your shredded cheddar cheese and keep stirring.
8. Once the cheese has melted, add your parmesan cheese. Mix that in and stir until it melts.
9. Add your sour cream and mix that in.
10. Season with seasoning salt and paprika.
11. Top with more shredded cheddar cheese.
12. Add slats of butter on top and place into the oven on broil at 500 degrees for a few minutes to brown the top. Enjoy!

PARMESAN CRUSTED COD FISH

SERVINGS: 6   PREPPING TIME: 20 MIN   COOKING TIME: 30 MIN

INGREDIENTS

- 2 cups of Bread Crumbs
- 1 cup of Parmesan Cheese
- 1 tbsp of Parsley
- 1 tbsp of Old Bay Seasoning
- 1 tbsp of Garlic Powder
- 1 tsp of Salt
- 1 tsp of Black Pepper
- 3 Eggs
- 6 Cod Fish Fillets
- 1 cup of olive oil

DIRECTIONS

1. In a large bowl, mix the bread crumbs, parmesan cheese, parsley, old bay seasoning and garlic powder.
2. In separate large bowl, add your egg and season with salt and pepper, and scramble.
3. Roll your cod fish into the egg mixture and then roll the fish into the bread crumb mixture. Set the fillets to the side.
4. In a hot pan on medium heat, add your olive oil.
5. Brown each fillet on each side for 3 to 5 minutes.
6. Once they're brown, place them onto your baking sheet.
7. Place into the oven at 375 degrees for 30 minutes.
8. Sprinkle them with lemon juice and serve!

LEMON PEPPER WINGS

SERVINGS: 6   PREPPING TIME: 20 MIN   COOKING TIME: 20 MIN

INGREDIENTS

- 1 tbsp of Salt
- 2 tbsp of Lemon Pepper
- 1 tbsp of Paprika
- 1 tbsp of Granulated Garlic
- 1/2 cup of Butter
- 1 tbsp of Garlic Powder
- 1 tbsp of Lemon Juice
- 1 tbsp of Chicken Broth
- 1 tsp of Black Pepper
- 1 tsp of Italian Seasoning
- 25 wingettes

DIRECTIONS

1. In a bowl, season your wings with salt, paprika, granulated garlic, and lemon pepper. Mix well.
2. Place onto a baking sheet and bake them at 400 degrees for 1 hour and 15 minutes.
3. In a hot pan on low heat, melt your butter. Now season with garlic powder. Stir.
4. Add your lemon juice and stir.
5. Add your chicken broth and stir.
6. Add your black pepper and italian seasoning and stir. Set your sauce to the side.
7. Remove your wings from the oven and place the wings into a bowl.
8. Pour your sauce onto the wings and mix well. Enjoy!

BAKED CHICKEN THIGHS W/ LEMON DIJON SAUCE

SERVINGS: 6   PREPPING TIME: 30 MIN   COOKING TIME: 60 M N

INGREDIENTS

- 1/2 cup of Butter
- 1 tbsp of Garlic Powder
- 1 tsp of Black Pepper
- 1 tsp of Lemon Juice
- 1 tsp of Chicken Broth
- 1 tbsp of Dijon Mustard
- 1 cup of Heavy Cream
- 12 bone in Chicken Thighs
- 1 tbsp of Olive Oil
- salt to taste

DIRECTIONS

1. In a hot pan on medium heat, pour a little olive oil into the pan.
2. Brown your thighs on each side for 3 to 5 minutes. Start skin side down.
3. Once you've brown the thighs, place them into your roasting pan.
4. Drizzle the oil from the pan over the thighs.
5. Cover and place into the oven at 375 degrees for 1 hour.
6. For the sauce, melt your butter into a hot pan on low heat.
7. Add the garlic powder, pepper and lemon juice. Stir.
8. Add the chicken broth and Dijon mustard. Stir.
9. Gradually add heavy cream to the sauce. Salt and pepper to taste. Stir and set to the side.
10. Remove your chicken from the oven and drizzle that sauce over the chicken. Enjoy!

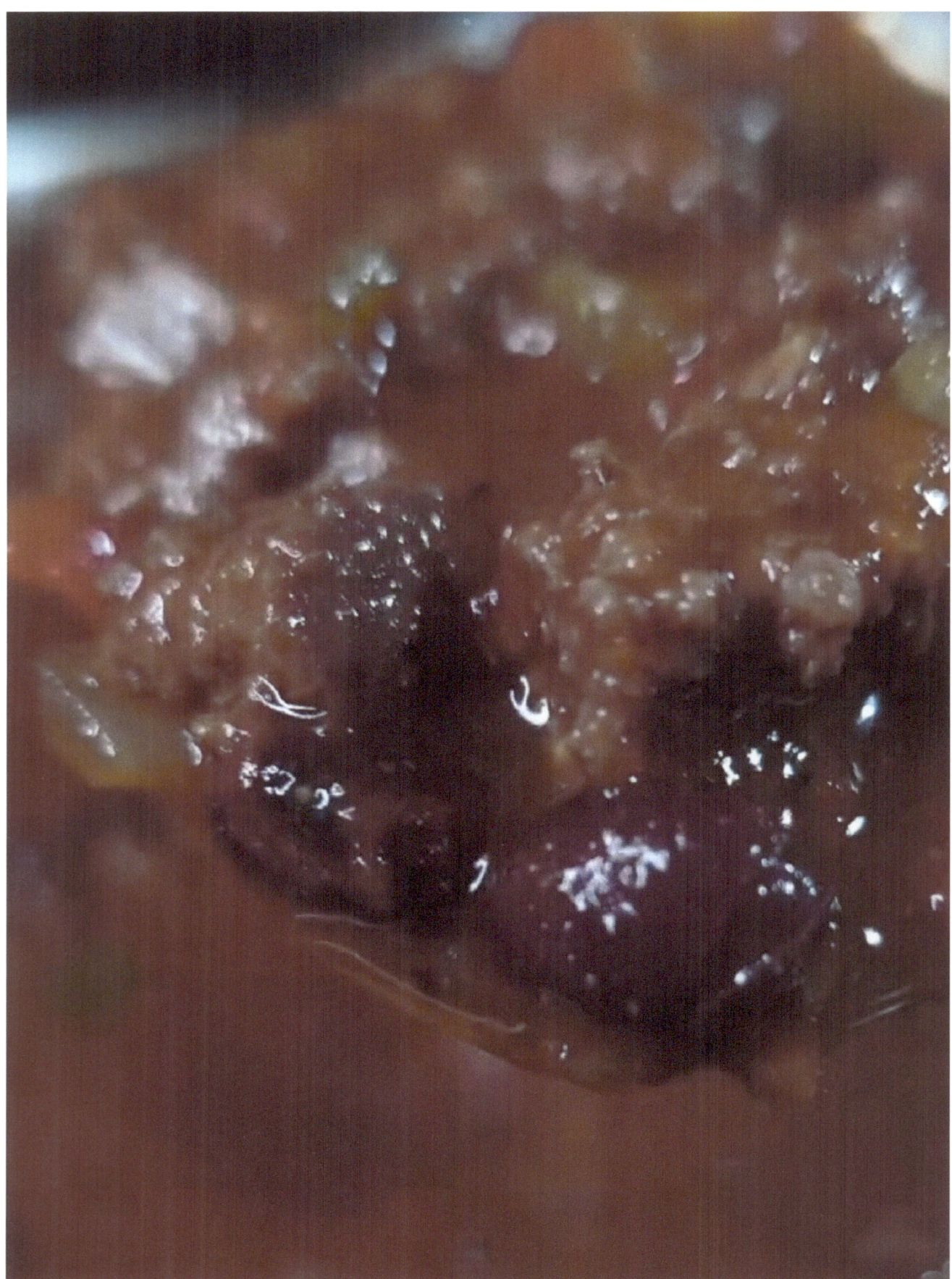

HOMEMADE CHILI

SERVINGS: 6 PREPPING TIME: 20 MIN COOKING TIME: 60 MIN

INGREDIENTS

- 2 lbs of Ground Beef
- 2 packages of Mild Chili Seasoning
- 1 tbsp of Salt
- 1 tbsp of Black Pepper
- 1 tbsp of Cumin
- 1 tbsp of Cocoa Powder
- 1 tbsp of Sugar
- 2 -28 oz cans of Crushed Tomatoes
- 2 -15 oz cans of Black Beans
- 3 tbsp of Beef Boullion
- 4 cups of Water
- 1 Onion (diced)
- 1 Green Pepper (diced)

DIRECTIONS

1. In a hot pan on medium heat, saute your onions and green peppers. Set that to the side.
2. In a large pot on medium heat, brown your ground beef.
3. Add you chili seasoning, salt, pepper, cumin, cocoa powder, and sugar. Stir well.
4. Add your crushed tomatoes, black beans and beef boullion. Stir well.
5. Add the water and diced onion and green peppers.
6. Bring that to a boil.
7. Cover and turn your heat to low. Let it simmer for one hour. Enjoy!

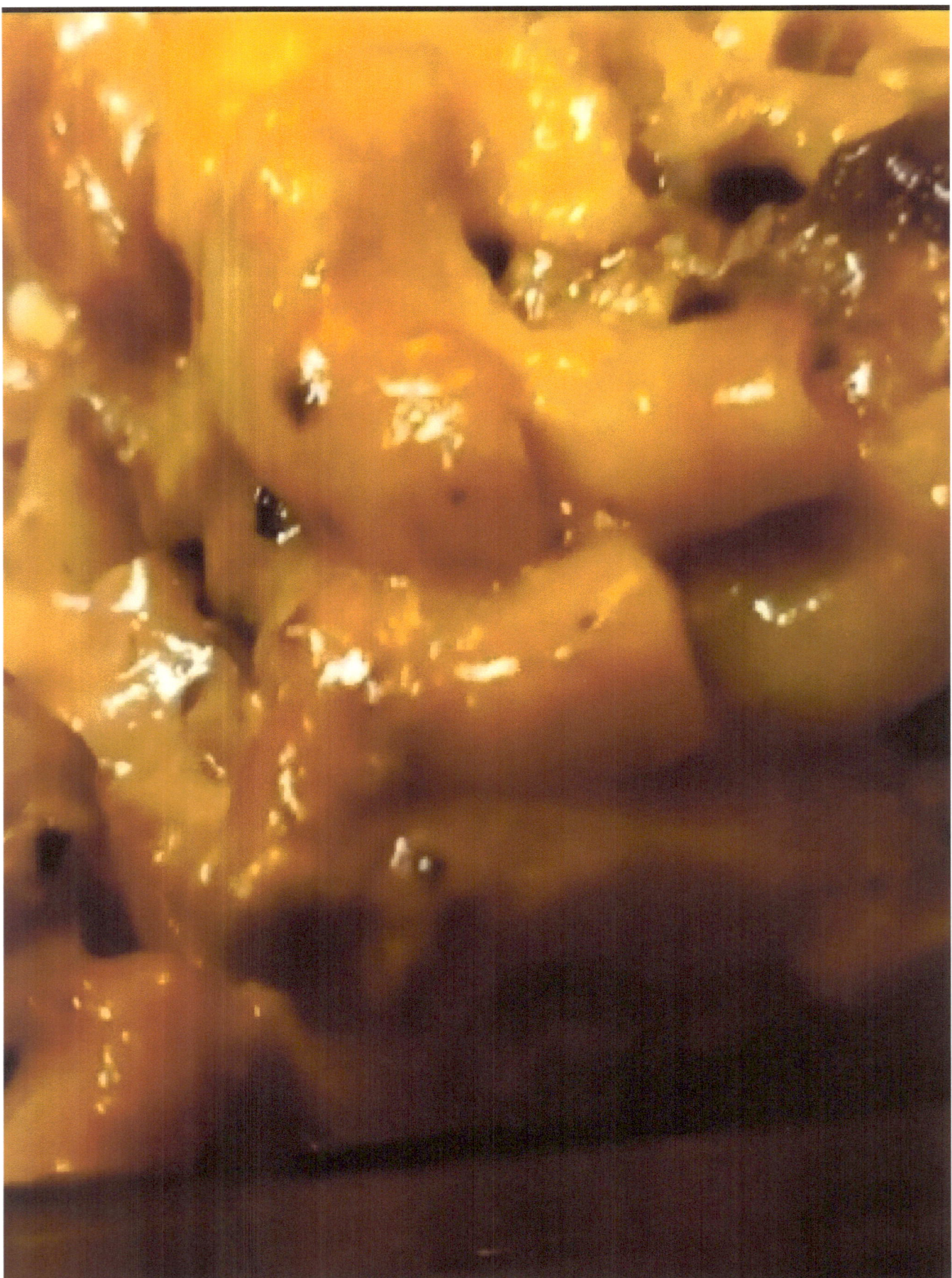

BEEF AND MACARONI

SERVINGS: 6   PREPPING TIME: 30 MIN   COOKING TIME: 30 MIN

INGREDIENTS

- 2 cups of cooked Macaroni noodles
- 1 Onion (diced)
- 1 lb of Ground Beef
- 1 tbsp of minced Garlic
- 1 tbsp of Oregano
- 1 tbsp of Black Pepper
- 1 tbsp of Basil
- 1 tbsp of Salt
- 1 -14 oz can of Diced Tomatoes
- 1 -14 oz can of Tomato Sauce
- 8 oz of Velveeta Cheese
- 1 cup of Shredded Cheddar Cheese

DIRECTIONS

1. In a hot pan on medium heat, brown your beef.
2. Add the minced garlic and onion. Saute.
3. Now add the oregano, black pepper, basil and salt. Saute.
4. Now add the diced tomatoes and the tomato sauce. Stir.
5. Add the cooked macaroni noodles and the Velveeta cheese.
6. Pour that mixture into a casserole dish and top with the shredded cheddar cheese.
7. Broil in the oven at 500 degrees for a just a few minutes to brown the top. Enjoy!

Thank You!

FOR PURCHASING MY COOKBOOK! I HOPE YOU ENJOY ALL OF THE RECIPES!

Follow Cooking with Tenny on

FACEBOOK | YOUTUBE | INSTAGRAM

"COOKING IS LIKE LOVE. IT SHOULD BE ENTERED INTO WITH ABANDON OR NOT AT ALL."
– HARRIET VAN HORNE

"A RECIPE HAS NO SOUL. YOU AS THE COOK MUST BRING SOUL TO THE RECIPE."
– THOMAS KELLER

"COOKING IS LIKE PAINTING OR WRITING A SONG. JUST AS THERE ARE ONLY SO MANY NOTES OR COLORS, THERE ARE ONLY SO MANY FLAVORS—IT'S HOW YOU COMBINE THEM THAT SETS YOU APART."
– WOLFGANG PUCK

"IF YOU ARE A CHEF, NO MATTER HOW GOOD A CHEF YOU ARE, IT'S NOT GOOD COOKING FOR YOURSELF; THE JOY IS IN COOKING FOR OTHERS. IT'S THE SAME WITH MUSIC."
– WILL.I.AM

"COOKING WITH KIDS IS NOT JUST ABOUT INGREDIENTS, RECIPES, AND COOKING. IT'S ABOUT HARNESSING IMAGINATION, EMPOWERMENT, AND CREATIVITY."
– GUY FIERI

"REAL COOKING IS MORE ABOUT FOLLOWING YOUR HEART THAN FOLLOWING RECIPES."
– UNKNOWN

"COOKING IS AT ONCE CHILD'S PLAY AND ADULT JOY. AND COOKING DONE WITH CARE IS AN ACT OF LOVE."
– CRAIG CLAIBORNE

"SO WHEN PEOPLE ASK ME, 'WHAT DO YOU THINK OF MICHELIN?' I DON'T COOK FOR GUIDES. I COOK FOR CUSTOMERS."
– GORDON RAMSAY

"COOKING IS NOT DIFFICULT. EVERYONE HAS TASTE, EVEN IF THEY DON'T REALIZE IT. EVEN IF YOU'RE NOT A GREAT CHEF, THERE'S NOTHING TO STOP YOU UNDERSTANDING THE DIFFERENCE BETWEEN WHAT TASTES GOOD AND WHAT DOESN'T."
– GERARD DEPARDIEU

"COOKING REQUIRES CONFIDENT GUESSWORK AND IMPROVISATION—EXPERIMENTATION AND SUBSTITUTION, DEALING WITH FAILURE AND UNCERTAINTY IN A CREATIVE WAY."
– PAUL THEROUX

"THE ONLY REAL STUMBLING BLOCK IS FEAR OF FAILURE. IN COOKING, YOU'VE GOT TO HAVE A WHAT-THE-HELL ATTITUDE."
– JULIA CHILD

"COOKING DEMANDS ATTENTION, PATIENCE, AND ABOVE ALL, A RESPECT FOR THE GIFTS OF THE EARTH. IT IS A FORM OF WORSHIP, A WAY OF GIVING THANKS."
– JUDITH B. JONES

www.ingramcontent.com/pod-product-compliance
Lightning Source LLC
Chambersburg PA
CBHW051837210526
45473CB00005B/1910